OWL AT HOME

A guide for the book by Arnold Lobel
Great Works Author: Tracy Pearce

Publishing Credits

Owen Pearce, *Contributing Author*; Robin Erickson, *Production Director*;
Lee Aucoin, *Creative Director*; Timothy J. Bradley, *Illustration Manager*;
Emily R. Smith, M.A.Ed., *Editorial Director*; Amber Goff, *Editorial Assistant*;
Don Tran, *Production Supervisor*; Corinne Burton, M.A.Ed., *Publisher*

Image Credits

Grace Alba (cover, page 11); Timothy J. Bradley (pages 60–62, page 70)

Standards

© 2007 Teachers of English to Speakers of Other Languages, Inc. (TESOL)
© 2007 Board of Regents of the University of Wisconsin System. World-Class Instructional Design and Assessment (WIDA)
© Copyright 2010. National Governors Association Center for Best Practices and Council of Chief State School Officers. All rights reserved.

Shell Education
5301 Oceanus Drive
Huntington Beach, CA 92649-1030
http://www.shelleducation.com
ISBN 978-1-4258-8957-9
© 2014 Shell Educational Publishing, Inc.

The classroom teacher may reproduce copies of materials in this book for classroom use only. The reproduction of any part for an entire school or school system is strictly prohibited. No part of this publication may be transmitted, stored, or recorded in any form without written permission from the publisher.

Table of contents

How to Use This Literature Guide 4
    Theme Thoughts 4
    Vocabulary 5
    Analyzing the Literature 6
    Reader Response 6
    Guided Close Reading 6
    Making Connections 7
    Language Learning 7
    Story Elements 7
    Culminating Activity 8
    Comprehension Assessment 8
    Response to Literature 8

Correlation to the Standards 8
    Purpose and Intent of Standards 8
    How to Find Standards Correlations 8
    Standards Correlation Chart 9
    TESOL and WIDA Standards 10

About the Author—Arnold Lobel 11
    Possible Texts for Text Comparisons 11

Book Summary of *Owl at Home* 12
    Cross-Curricular Connection 12
    Possible Texts for Text Sets 12

Teacher Plans and Student Pages 13
    Pre-Reading Theme Thoughts 13
    Section 1: "The Guest" 14
    Section 2: "Strange Bumps" 23
    Section 3: "Tear-Water Tea" 32
    Section 4: "Upstairs and Downstairs" 41
    Section 5: "Owl and the Moon" 50

Post-Reading Activities 59
    Post-Reading Theme Thoughts 59
    Culminating Activity: Stick Puppets and Reader's Theater 60
    Comprehension Assessment 65
    Response to Literature: Lessons for Owl 67

Writing Paper 70
Answer Key 71

Introduction

How to Use This Literature Guide

Today's standards demand rigor and relevance in the reading of complex texts. The units in this series guide teachers in a rich and deep exploration of worthwhile works of literature for classroom study. The most rigorous instruction can also be interesting and engaging!

Many current strategies for effective literacy instruction have been incorporated into these instructional guides for literature. Throughout the units, text-dependent questions are used to determine comprehension of the book as well as student interpretation of the vocabulary words. The books chosen for the series are complex and are exemplars of carefully crafted works of literature. Close reading is used throughout the units to guide students toward revisiting the text and using textual evidence to respond to prompts orally and in writing. Students must analyze the story elements in multiple assignments for each section of the book. All of these strategies work together to rigorously guide students through their study of literature.

The next few pages describe how to use this guide for a purposeful and meaningful literature study. Each section of this guide is set up in the same way to make it easier for you to implement the instruction in your classroom.

Theme Thoughts

The great works of literature used throughout this series have important themes that have been relevant to people for many years. Many of the themes will be discussed during the various sections of this instructional guide. However, it would also benefit students to have independent time to think about the key themes of the book.

Before students begin reading, have them complete the *Pre-Reading Theme Thoughts* (page 13). This graphic organizer will allow students to think about the themes outside the context of the story. They'll have the opportunity to evaluate statements based on important themes and defend their opinions. Be sure to keep students' papers for comparison to the *Post-Reading Theme Thoughts* (page 59). This graphic organizer is similar to the pre-reading activity. However, this time, students will be answering the questions from the point of view of one of the characters in the book. They have to think about how the character would feel about each statement and defend their thoughts. To conclude the activity, have students compare what they thought about the themes before they read the book to what the characters discovered during the story.

How to Use This Literature Guide (cont.)

Vocabulary

Each teacher reference vocabulary overview page has definitions and sentences about how key vocabulary words are used in the section. These words should be introduced and discussed with students. Students will use these words in different activities throughout the book.

On some of the vocabulary student pages, students are asked to answer text-related questions about vocabulary words from the sections. The following question stems will help you create your own vocabulary questions if you'd like to extend the discussion.

- How does this word describe _____'s character?
- How does this word connect to the problem in this story?
- How does this word help you understand the setting?
- Tell me how this word connects to the main idea of this story.
- What visual pictures does this word bring to your mind?
- Why do you think the author used this word?

At times, you may find that more work with the words will help students understand their meanings and importance. These quick vocabulary activities are a good way to further study the words.

- Students can play vocabulary concentration. Make one set of cards that has the words on them and another set with the definitions. Then, have students lay them out on the table and play concentration. The goal of the game is to match vocabulary words with their definitions. For early readers or English language learners, the two sets of cards could be the words and pictures of the words.
- Students can create word journal entries about the words. Students choose words they think are important and then describe why they think each word is important within the book. Early readers or English language learners could instead draw pictures about the words in a journal.
- Students can create puppets and use them to act out the vocabulary words from the stories. Students may also enjoy telling their own character-driven stories using vocabulary words from the original stories.

Introduction

How to Use This Literature Guide (cont.)

Analyzing the Literature

After you have read each section with students, hold a small-group or whole-class discussion. Provided on the teacher reference page for each section are leveled questions. The questions are written at two levels of complexity to allow you to decide which questions best meet the needs of your students. The Level 1 questions are typically less abstract than the Level 2 questions. These questions are focused on the various story elements, such as character, setting, and plot. Be sure to add further questions as your students discuss what they've read. For each question, a few key points are provided for your reference as you discuss the book with students.

Reader Response

In today's classrooms, there are often great readers who are below average writers. So much time and energy is spent in classrooms getting students to read on grade level that little time is left to focus on writing skills. To help teachers include more writing in their daily literacy instruction, each section of this guide has a literature-based reader response prompt. Each of the three genres of writing is used in the reader responses within this guide: narrative, informative/explanatory, and opinion. Before students write, you may want to allow them time to draw pictures related to the topic. Book-themed writing paper is provided on page 70 if your students need more space to write.

Guided Close Reading

Within each section of this guide, it is suggested that you closely reread a portion of the text with your students. Page numbers are given, but since some versions of the books may have different page numbers, the sections to be reread are described by location as well. After rereading the section, there are a few text-dependent questions to be answered by students. Working space has been provided to help students prepare for the group discussion. They should record their thoughts and ideas on the activity page and refer to it during your discussion. Rather than just taking notes, you may want to require students to write complete responses to the questions before discussing them with you.

Encourage students to read one question at a time and then go back to the text and discover the answer. Work with students to ensure that they use the text to determine their answers rather than making unsupported inferences. Suggested answers are provided in the answer key.

How to Use This Literature Guide (cont.)

Guided Close Reading (cont.)

The generic open-ended stems below can be used to write your own text-dependent questions if you would like to give students more practice.

- What words in the story support . . . ?
- What text helps you understand . . . ?
- Use the book to tell why _____ happens.
- Based on the events in the story, . . . ?
- Show me the part in the text that supports . . . .
- Use the text to tell why . . . .

Making Connections

The activities in this section help students make cross-curricular connections to mathematics, science, social studies, fine arts, or other curricular areas. These activities require higher-order thinking skills from students but also allow for creative thinking.

Language Learning

A special section has been set aside to connect the literature to language conventions. Through these activities, students will have opportunities to practice the conventions of standard English grammar, usage, capitalization, and punctuation.

Story Elements

It is important to spend time discussing what the common story elements are in literature. Understanding the characters, setting, plot, and theme can increase students' comprehension and appreciation of the story. If teachers begin discussing these elements in early childhood, students will more likely internalize the concepts and look for the elements in their independent reading. Another very important reason for focusing on the story elements is that students will be better writers if they think about how the stories they read are constructed.

In the story elements activities, students are asked to create work related to the characters, setting, or plot. Consider having students complete only one of these activities. If you give students a choice on this assignment, each student can decide to complete the activity that most appeals to him or her. Different intelligences are used so that the activities are diverse and interesting to all students.

How to Use This Literature Guide (cont.)

Culminating Activity

At the end of this instructional guide is a creative culminating activity that allows students the opportunity to share what they've learned from reading the book. This activity is open ended so that students can push themselves to create their own great works within your language arts classroom.

Comprehension Assessment

The questions in this section require students to think about the book they've read as well as the words that were used in the book. Some questions are tied to quotations from the book to engage students and require them to think about the text as they answer the questions.

Response to Literature

Finally, students are asked to respond to the literature by drawing pictures and writing about the characters and stories. A suggested rubric is provided for teacher reference.

Correlation to the Standards

Shell Education is committed to producing educational materials that are research and standards based. As part of this effort, we have correlated all of our products to the academic standards of all 50 states, the District of Columbia, the Department of Defense Dependents Schools, and all Canadian provinces.

Purpose and Intent of Standards

Standards are designed to focus instruction and guide adoption of curricula. Standards are statements that describe the criteria necessary for students to meet specific academic goals. They define the knowledge, skills, and content students should acquire at each level. Standards are also used to develop standardized tests to evaluate students' academic progress. Teachers are required to demonstrate how their lessons meet standards. Standards are used in the development of all of our products, so educators can be assured they meet high academic standards.

How To Find Standards Correlations

To print a customized correlation report of this product for your state, visit our website at http://www.shelleducation.com and follow the online directions. If you require assistance in printing correlation reports, please contact our Customer Service Department at 1-877-777-3450.

correlation to the standards (cont.)

standards correlation chart

The lessons in this book were written to support the Common Core College and Career Readiness Anchor Standards. The following chart indicates which lessons address the anchor standards.

Common Core College and Career Readiness Anchor Standard	Section
CCSS.ELA-Literacy.CCRA.R.1—Read closely to determine what the text says explicitly and to make logical inferences from it; cite specific textual evidence when writing or speaking to support conclusions drawn from the text.	Guided Close Reading Sections 1–5; Story Elements Sections 1, 3–4
CCSS.ELA-Literacy.CCRA.R.2—Determine central ideas or themes of a text and analyze their development; summarize the key supporting details and ideas.	Analyzing the Literature Sections 1–5; Post-Reading Theme Thoughts; Post-Reading Response to Literature
CCSS.ELA-Literacy.CCRA.R.3—Analyze how and why individuals, events, or ideas develop and interact over the course of a text.	Analyzing the Literature Sections 1–5; Guided Close Reading Sections 1–5; Story Elements Section 5; Post-Reading Response to Literature
CCSS.ELA-Literacy.CCRA.R.4—Interpret words and phrases as they are used in a text, including determining technical, connotative, and figurative meanings, and analyze how specific word choices shape meaning or tone.	Vocabulary Sections 1–5; Guided Close Reading Sections 1–5; Language Learning Section 2
CCSS.ELA-Literacy.CCRA.R.5—Analyze the structure of texts, including how specific sentences, paragraphs, and larger portions of the text (e.g., a section, chapter) relate to each other and the whole.	Vocabulary Sections 1–5; Guided Close Reading Sections 1–5
CCSS.ELA-Literacy.CCRA.R.9—Analyze how two or more texts address similar themes or topics in order to build knowledge or to compare the approaches the authors take.	Making Connections Section 5
CCSS.ELA-Literacy.CCRA.W.1—Write arguments to support claims in an analysis of substantive topics or texts using valid reasoning and relevant and sufficient evidence.	Reader Response Sections 4–5; Post-Reading Theme Thoughts
CCSS.ELA-Literacy.CCRA.W.2—Write informative/explanatory texts to examine and convey complex ideas and information clearly and accurately through the effective selection, organization, and analysis of content.	Reader Response Section 2

Introduction

Correlation to the Standards (cont.)

Standards Correlation Chart (cont.)

Common Core College and Career Readiness Anchor Standard	Section
CCSS.ELA-Literacy.CCRA.W.3—Write narratives to develop real or imagined experiences or events using effective technique, well-chosen details and well-structured event sequences.	Reader Response Sections 1, 3; Story Elements Sections 1–4; Language Learning Section 1
CCSS.ELA-Literacy.CCRA.W.4—Read and comprehend complex literary and informational texts independently and proficiently.	Entire Unit
CCSS.ELA-Literacy.CCRA.L.1—Demonstrate command of the conventions of standard English grammar and usage when writing or speaking.	Guided Close Reading Sections 1–5; Story Elements 3–4; Making Connections Section 1; Language Learning Sections 1–5
CCSS.ELA-Literacy.CCRA.L.3—Apply knowledge of language to understand how language functions in different contexts, to make effective choices for meaning or style, and to comprehend more fully when reading or listening.	Analyzing the Literature Sections 1–5; Guided Close Reading Sections 1–5; Story Elements Section 2; Making Connections Section 4
CCSS.ELA-Literacy.CCRA.L.4—Determine or clarify the meaning of unknown and multiple-meaning words and phrases by using context clues, analyzing meaningful word parts, and consulting general and specialized reference materials, as appropriate.	Vocabulary Sections 1–5; Making Connections Section 4
CCSS.ELA-Literacy.CCRA.L.6—Acquire and use accurately a range of general academic and domain-specific words and phrases sufficient for reading, writing, speaking, and listening at the college and career readiness level; demonstrate independence in gathering vocabulary knowledge when encountering an unknown term important to comprehension or expression.	Vocabulary Sections 1–5

TESOL and WIDA Standards

The lessons in this book promote English language development for English language learners. The following TESOL and WIDA English Language Development Standards are addressed through the activities in this book:

- **Standard 1:** English language learners communicate for social and instructional purposes within the school setting.
- **Standard 2:** English language learners communicate information, ideas and concepts necessary for academic success in the content area of language arts.

Introduction

About the Author—Arnold Lobel

Arnold Lobel was born on May 22, 1933, in Los Angeles, California. He grew up in Schenectady, New York. As a young boy, Lobel enjoyed reading and drawing. He attended art school and married Anita Kempler, who illustrated children's books.

Once he graduated, Lobel began to work in advertising. He did not enjoy working in that environment. He wanted to do something creative. However, there were not many successful children's authors at that time. Lobel decided to try illustrating children's books first. After many visits to publishers, Harper and Row gave him a chance. After awhile, he also began writing books in order to better support his family financially.

Lobel stated in multiple interviews that he was not very confident about his writing. However, he was confident in his artistic ability. His work was first published in 1958, and he continued to be published until he died in 1987. His daughter, Adrianna, pulled together books of his work that have been published posthumously.

In 1981, he won the Caldecott Medal for *Fables*, which he authored and illustrated. His 1972 book, *Frog and Toad Together* is a Newbery Award Honor book. *Frog and Toad Are Friends* is a Caldecott Award Honor book.

Possible Texts for Text Comparisons

The *Frog and Toad* series, *Mouse Tales*, and *Mouse Soup* are books by the same author that could be used for enriching text comparisons.

Introduction

Book Summary of *Owl at Home*

Owl at Home consists of five short tales that follow Owl through a series of adventures in his own home. Owl is very innocent but somewhat silly and childlike as he explores the world around him. Life lessons are taught with simple words in this entertaining book. Arnold Lobel allows the readers to see through the confusion even as Owl fails to learn the lesson. Students will love the antics of Owl and his misunderstandings.

In *Owl at Home*, five different stories introduce readers to the innocent, silly actions of Owl.

- In "The Guest," Owl invites winter into his home to sit by the fire. Owl is very shocked when his houseguest does not behave.
- In "Strange Bumps," Owl becomes angry when he finds strange bumps at the end of his bed, underneath the covers. Owl cannot figure out where they came from or why they will not leave.
- Melancholy Owl makes a pot of tea in "Tear-Water Tea." Owl recalls many sad things and fills the kettle with his tears to make tear-water tea.
- "Upstairs and Downstairs" is a funny story about Owl living in a two-story house. He wonders if he can be up and down at the same time by running up and down as fast as he can. After his frustration he finds a clever solution.
- In "Owl and the Moon," Owl goes for a walk, and he makes a friend who follows him all the way home.

Cross-Curricular Connection

This book can be used in a science unit on the study of owls or in a social studies unit on different types of friends.

Possible Texts for Text Sets

- Gibbons, Gail. *Owls*. Holiday House, 2006.
- Hutchins, Pat. *Good-Night Owl!* Aladdin Paperbacks, 1990.
- Waddell, Martin. *Owl Babies*. Candlewick Press, 1996.
- Yolen, Jane. *Owl Moon*. Penguin Putnam Books for Young Readers, 1987.

or

- Heine, Helme. *Friends*. Aladdin Paperbacks, 1997.
- Hoban, Russell. *A Bargain for Frances*. HarperCollins, 2003.
- Kellogg, Steven. *Best Friends*. Puffin, 1992.
- Willems, Mo. *There Is a Bird on Your Head!* Disney-Hyperion, 2007.

Name _____

Introduction

Pre-Reading Theme Thoughts

Directions: Read each statement. Draw a picture of a happy face or a sad face. The face should show how you feel about the statement. Then, use words to say why you feel this way.

Statement	How Do You Feel? ☺ ☹	Why Do You Feel That Way?
It is wonderful to have a friend.		
There are many joyful things to think of in life.		
Feelings are important to have.		
It is hard to say good-bye to a friend.		

Teacher Plans—Section 1 "The Guest"

Vocabulary Overview

Key words and phrases from this section are provided below with definitions and sentences about how the words are used in the story. Introduce and discuss these important vocabulary words with the students. If you think these words or other words in the story warrant more time devoted to them, there are suggestions in the introduction for other vocabulary activities (page 5).

Word	Definition	Sentence about Text
supper (p. 5)	the evening meal	Owl is eating **supper** by the fire.
banging (p. 6)	hitting something in a way that makes a loud noise	Owl hears a **banging** at his door.
wind (p. 6)	a natural movement of air	The **wind** is blowing outside when Owl opens the door.
kind (p. 8)	showing a gentle nature and a desire to help others	Owl is **kind** and lets the winter come in where it is warm.
wide (p. 9)	very big from side to side	Owl opens the door very **wide**.
blew out (p. 11)	to extinguish or put out by a gust of air	Naughty Winter **blows out** the fire in the fireplace.
whirled (p. 13)	turned rapidly in circles	The snow **whirls** up the stairs.
guest (p. 13)	a person who is invited to visit or stay in someone's home	Winter is Owl's **guest**, and it should behave itself.
window shades (p. 13)	a roll of cloth or plastic that is hung at the top of a window and that can be pulled down to cover the window	The **window shades** flap and shiver.
flap (p. 13)	to move up and down or back and forth	Winter makes the window shades **flap**.

Name _____

"The Guest"

Vocabulary Activity

Directions: Choose at least two words from the story. Draw a picture that shows what these words mean. Label your picture.

Words from the Story

| supper | banging | wind | kind | wide |
| blew out | whirled | guest | window shades | flap |

Directions: Answer this question

1. Who is **banging** at the door?
_____
_____

15

Teacher Plans—Section 1 "The Guest"

Analyzing the Literature

Provided below are discussion questions you can use in small groups, with the whole class, or for written assignments. Each question is written at two levels so you can choose the right question for each group of students. For each question, a few key points are provided for your reference as you discuss the book with students.

Story Element	Level 1	Level 2	Key Discussion Points
Plot	What things does Winter do when it enters Owl's home?	How do the illustrations help you to find out what things Winter does when it enters Owl's home?	Winter comes into Owl's home and runs around the house. Winter blows out the fire in the fireplace. Snow whirls up the stairs and down the hallway and covers everything. Winter makes the window shades flap and even turns the pea soup into hard, green ice.
Plot	What is the problem in this story?	Describe the problem and solution in this story.	The problem is that Owl lets Winter come into his house, and Winter does not behave. Owl orders Winter out of his house and tells Winter not to come back. Owl makes his room warm again and finishes his supper.
Setting	Describe the setting of the story.	What is the most interesting part of the setting of the story?	The setting is Owl's home. This includes the front of his home and the upstairs and downstairs inside his home. The setting also includes the food that Owl is eating and the fire in the fireplace.
Character	What does Owl say to his guest, Winter?	Describe how Owl reacts to his guest, Winter.	Owl tells Winter that this is no way to behave. Owl tells Winter that it must go. He also tells it not to come back.

Name _____

"The Guest"

Reader Response

Think

In "The Guest," Owl deals with a lot of snow. Think about a time you were in bad weather. Maybe you saw pouring rain or a snowstorm.

Narrative Writing Prompt

Write about a time you had to deal with really bad weather.

"The Guest"

Name _____

Guided Close Reading

Closely reread pages 6–7. This is where Owl hears a loud sound at the front door.

Directions: Think about these questions. In the chart, write ideas or draw pictures as you think. Be ready to share your answers.

_____

❶ Which words help you to predict who is actually at Owl's door?

_____

❷ What words describe the noises that Owl hears at his door?

_____

❸ Use the text to tell where Owl sits again after opening the door.

Name _____

"The Guest"

Making Connections—Will It Blow?

Directions: A cold wind comes into Owl's home. It blows around and around. Think about each item below. Make a prediction about if each item can be blown by the wind. Then, use a fan to act as the wind. Test each prediction. Write the result after each item is tested.

Item to be Tested	Prediction	Result
crayon		
stapler		
leaf		
feather		
block		
straw		

© Shell Education

#40009—Instructional Guide: Owl at Home

"The Guest"

Name _____

Language Learning—Poetry

Directions: Poetry is a great way to share ideas. Write a poem about how Winter acts when it comes into Owl's home. Draw a picture to illustrate your poem.

Name _____

"The Guest"

Story Elements—Character

Directions: Winter comes into Owl's house. It does many things that a guest should not do. Draw pictures of at least three of the naughty things that Winter does in Owl's house. Label each picture.

"The Guest"

Name _____

Story Elements—Plot

Directions: Write a new story about a guest in Owl's home. Choose a different character to be in the story instead of Winter. Owl's new guest might be a friend, family member, or even a pet.

_____

_____

_____

_____

_____

_____

_____

_____

_____

_____

_____

_____

_____

_____

Teacher Plans—Section 2 "Strange Bumps"

Vocabulary Overview

Key words and phrases from this section are provided below with definitions and sentences about how the words are used in the story. Introduce and discuss these important vocabulary words with the students. If you think these words or other words in the story warrant more time devoted to them, there are suggestions in the introduction for other vocabulary activities (page 5).

Word	Definition	Sentence about Text
candle (p. 19)	wax in a stick or other shape that has a string in the middle that can be burned	Owl blows out the **candle** and goes to sleep.
yawn (p. 19)	to open your mouth wide while taking in breath, usually because you are tired or bored	It is time for bed and Owl **yawns**.
strange (p. 19)	different from what is usual, normal, or expected	Owl sees two **strange** bumps at the bottom of his bed.
lifted up (p. 20)	to move up	Owl **lifts up** the blanket to look into the bed.
darkness (p. 20)	a state in which little or no light can be seen	Owl can see only **darkness**.
pleasant (p. 21)	causing a feeling of happiness or pleasure	Owl thinks it will not be **pleasant** if the bumps grow bigger.
moved (p. 22)	to cause something to go from one position to another	Owl **moves** his feet up and down.
other (p. 22)	different or separate from the thing that has already been mentioned	Owl sees the **other** bump moving.
crash (p. 27)	a very loud noise	The bed comes falling down with a **crash**.
safe (p. 28)	not in danger	Owl sleeps in his chair, where he feels **safe**.

"Strange Bumps"

Name _____

Vocabulary Activity

Directions: Draw a line to complete each sentence.

Beginnings of Sentences	Endings of Sentences
It is late,	up and down.
Owl blows out the **candle**	at the bottom of his bed.
Owl sees two **strange** bumps	to go to sleep.
The bumps **move**	and Owl yawns.
The bed falls down with a	**crash** and a bang.

Directions: Answer this question

1. In what **pleasant** place does Owl decide to sleep?

_____

_____

Teacher Plans—Section 2 "Strange Bumps"

Analyzing the Literature

Provided below are discussion questions you can use in small groups, with the whole class, or for written assignments. Each question is written at two levels so you can choose the right question for each group of students. For each question, a few key points are provided for your reference as you discuss the book with students.

Story Element	Level 1	Level 2	Key Discussion Points
Character	How does Owl feel about the strange bumps?	Describe how Owl feels about the strange bumps throughout the story.	Owl is scared of the two strange bumps. He does not know what they are and feels he will never get to sleep.
Character	What is a clue that tells us Owl is frightened?	Describe at least three clues that show us Owl is frightened.	Owl is trying to sleep, but he cannot. He is afraid the bumps will grow bigger. He jumps up and down on his bed. He runs down the stairs.
Plot	Why is this story called "Strange Bumps"?	What are details from the text that relate specifically to the title?	Owl sees two bumps at the bottom of his bed. He keeps wondering what the strange bumps are. The bumps keep moving, and they do not go away.
Plot	What is something that Owl does to try to figure out what the strange bumps are?	Describe the things that Owl does to figure out what the strange bumps are.	Owl moves his feet up and down. Owl pulls all the covers off his bed. He also jumps up and down on top of his bed.

"Strange Bumps"

Name _____

Reader Response

Think

In "Strange Bumps," Owl gets scared. Think about a time you were scared.

Informative/Explanatory Writing Prompt

Write about what to do if you get scared. How can you calm yourself down?

_____
_____
_____
_____
_____
_____
_____
_____
_____
_____
_____

Name _____

"Strange Bumps"

Guided Close Reading

Closely reread pages 22–23. This is when the bumps are moving.

Directions: Think about these questions. In the chart, write ideas or draw pictures as you think. Be ready to share your answers.

❶ Look at page 22 and describe what is moving up and down.

❷ Use the text and pictures to describe what Owl pulls off of his bed.

❸ Use words from the text to describe what Owl sees at the bottom of his bed.

"Strange Bumps"

Name _____

Making Connections—Who, What, When, and Where

Directions: Asking questions can help us to find details in a story. This can help us understand the story better. Write four good questions that can be answered by looking back at the story.

Who _____ ?

What _____ ?

When _____ ?

Where _____ ?

Name _____

"Strange Bumps"

Language Learning—Writing with Sensory Details

Directions: Sensory details are special words. They help readers see, hear, feel, taste, and smell the objects in a story. Look back at the story "Strange Bumps." Write a sensory word or phrase from the story in each box.

"Strange Bumps"

Name _____

Story Elements—Character

Directions: Owl is scared of the strange bumps. Write a lullaby (or song) that will help him to fall asleep.

Name _____

"Strange Bumps"

Story Elements—Setting

Directions: Choose your favorite scene from "Strange Bumps." Describe the setting of that scene in a poem.

This poem was written by

Teacher Plans—Section 3 "Tear-Water Tea"

Vocabulary Overview

Key words and phrases from this section are provided below with definitions and sentences about how the words are used in the story. Introduce and discuss these important vocabulary words with the students. If you think these words or other words in the story warrant more time devoted to them, there are suggestions in the introduction for other vocabulary activities (page 5).

Word	Definition	Sentence about Text
kettle (p. 31)	a container used for heating or boiling liquid	Owl takes the **kettle** out so he can make tea.
cupboard (p. 31)	a piece of furniture used for storage that has doors and contains shelves	The kettle is kept in the **cupboard**.
lap (p. 31)	the area between the knees and the hips of a person who is sitting down	Owl puts the kettle in his **lap**.
broken (p. 32)	separated into parts or pieces by being hit, damaged, etc.	Owl thinks of chairs with **broken** legs.
forgotten (p. 32)	unable to think of or remember something	There are songs that cannot be sung because the words have been **forgotten**.
behind (p. 33)	in or toward the back	If a spoon falls **behind** the stove you cannot reach it.
stove (p. 33)	a flat piece of kitchen equipment for cooking that usually has four devices, called burners, which become hot when they are turned on	Spoons have fallen behind the **stove** and are never seen again.
sobbed (p. 35)	cried noisily while taking in short, sudden breaths	Owl **sobs** while thinking about sad things.
filled up (p. 37)	became completely full	The kettle **fills up** with tears.
boil (p. 38)	when liquid becomes so hot that bubbles are formed and rise to the top	Owl puts the kettle on the stove to **boil** the tea.

Name _____

"Tear-Water Tea"

Vocabulary Activity

Directions: These sentences are from the story written by Arnold Lobel. Cut apart the sentence strips. Put the sentences in order. Use the story to help you.

"Soon the **kettle** was all **filled up** with tears."

"'Chairs with **broken** legs,' said Owl."

"Many large tears dropped into the **kettle**."

"Owl took the **kettle** out of the **cupboard**."

"He put the **kettle** on the **stove** to **boil** for tea."

"He put the **kettle** on his **lap**."

Teacher Plans—Section 3 "Tear-Water Tea"

Analyzing the Literature

Provided below are discussion questions you can use in small groups, with the whole class, or for written assignments. Each question is written at two levels so you can choose the right question for each group of students. For each question, a few key points are provided for your reference as you discuss the book with students.

Story Element	Level 1	Level 2	Key Discussion Points
Plot	What are some of the things that make Owl sad?	Describe at least three things that make Owl so sad.	Chairs with broken legs, songs with forgotten words, spoons lost behind the stove, books with torn-out pages, clocks that have stopped, mornings that no one sees, mashed potatoes left on a plate, and too-short pencils make Owl sad.
Character	Why does Owl make tear-water tea?	How do you know that the tear-water tea helps Owl?	Owl makes tear-water tea to help him with his sadness. He says that he feels happy as he fills his cup and the tea is always very good.
Character	How does Owl's mood change throughout the story?	Describe the difference in Owl's mood throughout the story.	In the very beginning of the story, Owl is neither sad, nor happy. Owl then becomes very sad as he thinks of many things that make him sad. At the very end, he is feeling happy as he drinks his tear-water tea.

Name _____

"Tear-Water Tea"

Reader Response

Think

In "Tear-Water Tea," Owl is very sad. Think about what makes you sad. Also, think about what makes you feel better.

Narrative Writing Prompt

Write about a time when you were very sad. Be sure to tell what helped make you feel better.

"Tear-Water Tea"

Name _____

Guided Close Reading

Closely reread the last two pages of the story (pages 38–39). This is when Owl drinks his tea.

Directions: Think about these questions. In the chart, write ideas or draw pictures as you think. Be ready to share your answers.

❶ What words in the story tell you how Owl feels at the end of "Tear-Water Tea"?

❷ Describe how the tea tastes to Owl.

❸ Based on the events of the story, why does Owl stop crying?

Name _____

"Tear-Water Tea"

Making connections— Things Recycled

Owl thinks of many sad things in this story. Some of the things he is sad about are items that are not being used. Many of the things that we throw away every day can be reused, recycled, or composted.

Directions: Draw a line from each item to the correct bin.

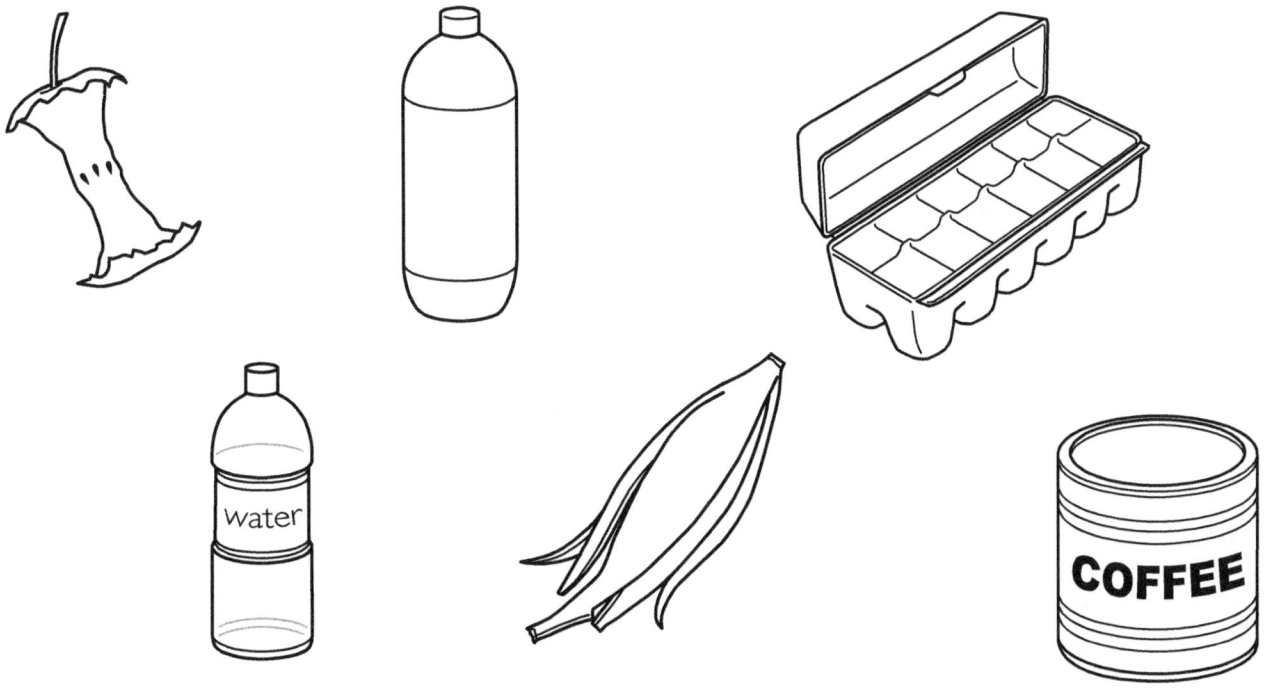

"Tear-Water Tea"

Name _____

Language Learning—Finding Nouns

Directions: Many things make Owl sad. These "things" are nouns. Draw pictures of four nouns that make Owl sad. Label each noun with its name.

Name _____

"Tear-Water Tea"

Story Elements—Setting

Directions: Using details and clues from the story, draw one of the settings from the story. Write at least two sentences describing your picture.

"Tear-Water Tea"

Name _____

Story Elements—Plot

Directions: Write a skit. Have yourself talk to Owl. What would you say to make him feel better?

You: _____

_____

Owl: _____

_____

You: _____

_____

Owl: _____

_____

You: _____

_____

Owl: _____

Teacher Plans—Section 4 "Upstairs and Downstairs"

Vocabulary Overview

Key words and phrases from this section are provided below with definitions and sentences about how the words are used in the story. Introduce and discuss these important vocabulary words with the students. If you think these words or other words in the story warrant more time devoted to them, there are suggestions in the introduction for other vocabulary activities (page 5).

Word	Definition	Sentence about Text
upstairs (p. 41)	the upper floors of a building	Owl's bedroom is **upstairs** in his house.
downstairs (p. 41)	the lower and usually main floor of a building	Owl's living room is **downstairs** in his house.
stairway (p. 41)	a set of stairs that joins one level or floor to another	There are 20 steps on Owl's **stairway**.
wonder (p. 42)	to think about something with curiosity	Owl says, "I **wonder** how my upstairs is?"
missing (p. 42)	to notice or feel the absence of something	Owl is always **missing** one place or the other.
faster (p. 44)	with great speed	Owl runs up and down the stairs **faster** and **faster**.
evening (p. 47)	the last part of the day and early part of the night	Owl runs up and down the stairs all **evening**.
at once (p. 47)	at the same time	Owl cannot be in both places **at once**.
tired (p. 49)	feeling a need to rest or sleep	Owl is very **tired**, and he wants to rest.
middle (p. 49)	equally distant from the ends or sides; halfway between two points	Owl sits right in the **middle** of the stairs.

"Upstairs and Downstairs"

Name _____

Vocabulary Activity

Directions: Complete each sentence below. Use one of the words listed.

Words from the Story

| downstairs | evening | at once | missing |

1. Sometimes Owl is _____ in his living room.

2. Owl is always _____ one place or another.

3. Owl runs upstairs and downstairs all _____.

4. Owl cannot be in both places _____.

Directions: Answer this question.

5. Why is Owl **tired**?

_____

_____

_____

_____

Teacher Plans—Section 4 "Upstairs and Downstairs"

Analyzing the Literature

Provided below are discussion questions you can use in small groups, with the whole class, or for written assignments. Each question is written at two levels so you can choose the right question for each group of students. For each question, a few key points are provided for your reference as you discuss the book with students.

Story Element	Level 1	Level 2	Key Discussion Points
Character	In what ways is Owl being silly in this story?	Describe whether you think Owl is being silly.	Owl is silly when he runs very fast so he can be in both places at once, when he calls to himself, and he keeps running up and down all evening.
Plot	What is the most exciting part of the story?	What is the problem in this story, and how does Owl solve it?	The problem is that Owl wants to be upstairs and downstairs at the same time. He says he is always missing one place or the other. Owl solves the problem by sitting in the middle of the stairway.
Plot	Who solves Owl's problem?	In what ways does the story's solution not really solve any problems?	Owl tries to solve his own problem when he sits in the middle of the stairway. However, the problem still exists because he cannot be upstairs and downstairs at the same time.
Setting	What is the setting of the story?	Describe the setting of the story.	The story takes place at the top of the stairs, at the bottom of the stairs, and on the stairs of Owl's home.

"Upstairs and Downstairs"

Name _____

Reader Response

Think

In "Upstairs and Downstairs," Owl can't make a decision. Think about what you do to help yourself make decisions.

Opinion Writing Prompt

What decision would you make if you were Owl? Would you stay upstairs or downstairs?

Name _____

"Upstairs and Downstairs"

Guided Close Reading

Closely reread pages 42–43. This is when Owl is running up and down the stairs.

Directions: Think about these questions. In the chart, write ideas or draw pictures as you think. Be ready to share your answers.

❶ Find evidence that tells what the problem in the story is.

❷ Use the text to tell why Owl wants to be upstairs and downstairs at the same time.

❸ How does Owl try to be upstairs and downstairs at the same time?

"Upstairs and Downstairs"

Name _____

Making Connections— Opposites Are Antonyms

Directions: *Upstairs* and *downstairs* are the opposite of each other. Two words that are opposites can also be called antonyms. Write the antonyms in the sentences below. Use the Word Bank.

Word Bank

| off | found | right | short | under | cold |

1. **Lost** is opposite of _____.

2. **Hot** is opposite of _____.

3. **Tall** is opposite of _____.

4. **Left** is opposite of _____.

5. **Over** is opposite of _____.

6. **On** is opposite of _____.

Name _____

"Upstairs and Downstairs"

Language Learning—Compound Words

Directions: A compound word is two words that join together to make a new word. This story has two compound words in the title! Match the words below to create compound words.

up	room
stair	stairs
down	way
bed	stairs

Directions: Write the compound words in ABC order.

_____

_____

_____

_____

_____

"Upstairs and Downstairs"

Name _____

Story Elements—Characters

Directions: Write an acrostic poem about Owl in this story. Use the first letter to start each line. Be sure each line describes Owl.

O _____

W _____

L _____

Name _____

"Upstairs and Downstairs"

Story Elements—Plot

Directions: Draw a picture predicting what you think will happen when Owl is done resting in the middle of the stairs. Write at least two sentences to go along with your picture.

_____
_____
_____
_____
_____

Teacher Plans—Section 5 "Owl and the Moon"

Vocabulary Overview

Key words and phrases from this section are provided below with definitions and sentences about how the words are used in the story. Introduce and discuss these important vocabulary words with the students. If you think these words or other words in the story warrant more time devoted to them, there are suggestions in the introduction for other vocabulary activities (page 5).

Word	Definition	Sentence about Text
seashore (p. 51)	the land along the edge of the sea that is usually covered with sand or rocks	Owl walks down to the **seashore**.
waves (p. 51)	an area of moving water that is raised above the main surface of the water	Owl looks out at the **waves**.
edge (p. 51)	the line or part where an object or area begins or ends	A tip of the moon comes up over the **edge** of the sea.
whole (p. 52)	complete or full	The moon is **whole** and round.
shining (p. 52)	producing or reflecting a bright, steady light	Soon, the moon is round and **shining**.
path (p. 54)	a track that is made by people or animals walking over the ground	Owl walks home down the **path**.
following (p. 54)	coming after or going behind	The moon is **following** Owl.
fine (p. 56)	very good	The moon looks so **fine** over the sea.
farther (p. 56)	to a more distant place or time or a more advanced point	Owl walks a little **farther**.
loudly (p. 58)	strongly and noticeably in sound	Owl shouts **loudly** to the moon.

Name _____

"Owl and the Moon"

Vocabulary Activity

Directions: Write at least two sentences using words from the story.

Words from the Story

seashore	waves	edge	whole	shining
path	following	fine	farther	loudly

_____

_____

_____

_____

_____

_____

Directions: Answer this question.

1. Why does Owl think the moon is **following** him?

_____

_____

_____

Teacher Plans—Section 5 "Owl and the Moon"

Analyzing the Literature

Provided below are discussion questions you can use in small groups, with the whole class, or for written assignments. Each question is written at two levels so you can choose the right question for each group of students. For each question, a few key points are provided for your reference as you discuss the book with students.

Story Element	Level 1	Level 2	Key Discussion Points
Character	How do you know that Owl is a good friend in this story?	In what ways does Owl show the moon that he is a good friend?	Owl says that they must be very good friends. He also says he will come back to see the moon again. Owl feels sad when he thinks the moon is gone.
Setting	Describe the setting of this story.	How is this setting different from the other Owl stories?	The setting takes place outside of Owl's home. All of the other stories took place inside of Owl's home. This setting changes from the seashore, to the path through the trees, and to the top of a hill.
Character	How does Owl feel at the very end of the story?	Describe how Owl's mood changes throughout the story.	Owl is happy at the beginning of the story as he talks with the moon. Then, Owl becomes sad as he says good-bye to the moon. Owl is happy again when the moon shines through his window.
Plot	Why does Owl think the moon is following him?	What are some clues that show why Owl thinks the moon is following him home?	Owl thinks the moon is looking at him. Then, the moon is still in the same place, even after Owl walks away.

Name _____

"Owl and the Moon"

Reader Response

Think

In "Owl and the Moon," Owl becomes friends with the moon. Think about a special friend that you have.

Opinion Writing Prompt

Write about what makes a good friend. What characteristics do you want your friends to have?

_____
_____
_____
_____
_____
_____
_____
_____
_____
_____
_____

"Owl and the Moon"

Name _____

Guided Close Reading

Closely reread pages 58–61. Owl is walking and the moon has gone behind some clouds.

Directions: Think about these questions. In the chart, write ideas or draw pictures as you think. Be ready to share your answers.

❶ Why does Owl shout at the moon?

❷ Use the book to tell why Owl thinks the moon is gone. Where has the moon really gone?

❸ What word on page 60 shows that Owl is feeling gloomy?

54 #40009—Instructional Guide: Owl at Home © Shell Education

Name _____

"Owl and the Moon"

Making connections— compare and contrast

Directions: Read the book *Mooncake* by Frank Asch. Then, reread "Owl and the Moon." Compare and contrast these two stories about the moon.

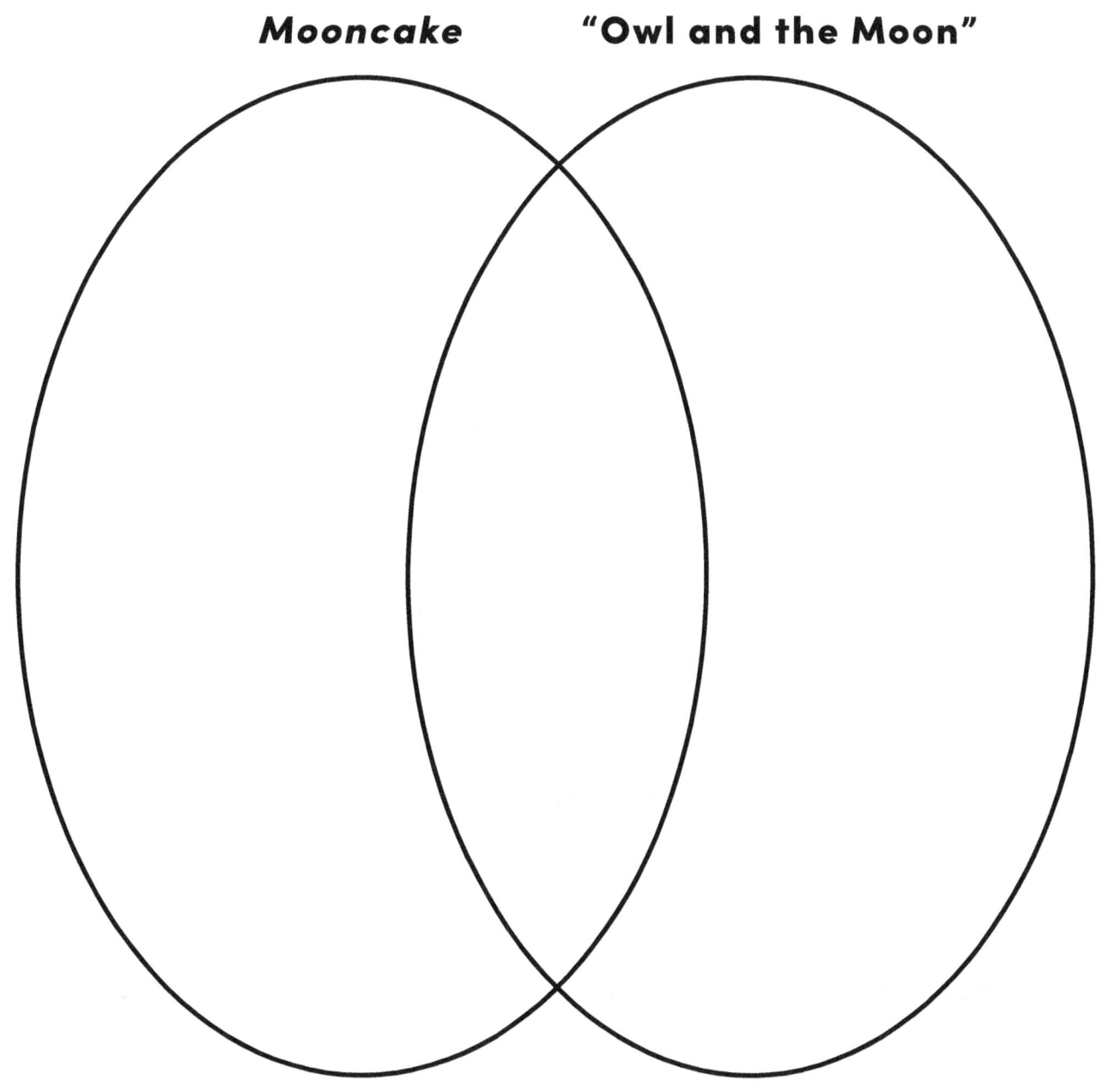

Mooncake   "Owl and the Moon"

"Owl and the Moon"

Name _____

Language Learning—Adjectives

Directions: Adjectives are words that describe things. It is very important to choose your words carefully. Below, write words that describe the moon.

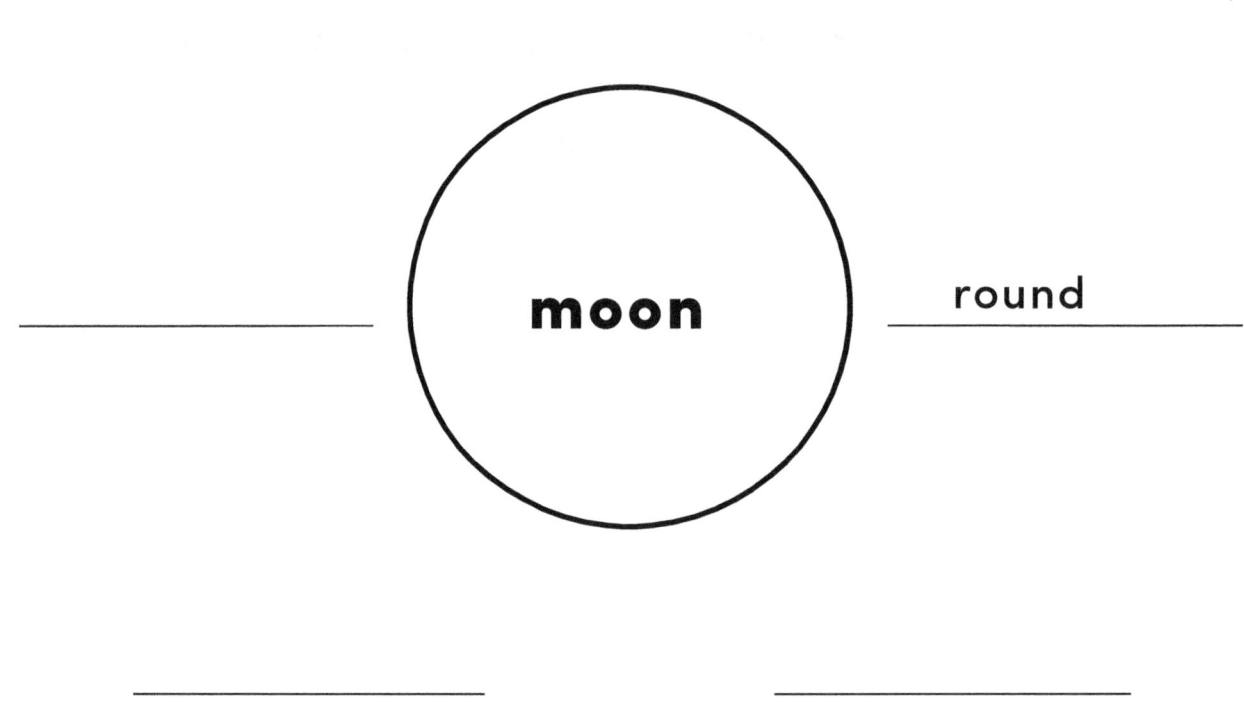

Directions: Write a comparison.

_____
- -

The moon is like _____ .

Name _____

"Owl and the Moon"

Story Elements—Characters

Directions: Draw a picture of the moon. Add a face to make it look friendly. Describe what you would like about being friends with the moon.

"Owl and the Moon"

Name _____

Story Elements—Plot

Directions: Make a list of at least five main events in the story.

_____

- _____

  _____

- _____

  _____

- _____

  _____

- _____

  _____

- _____

  _____

Post-Reading Theme Thoughts

Directions: Pretend you are Owl. Draw a picture of a happy face or a sad face to show how Owl would feel about each statement. Then use words to explain your picture.

Statement	How Does Owl Feel? 😊 ☹	Explain Owl's Answer
It is wonderful to have a friend.		
There are many joyful things to think of in life.		
It is hard to say good-bye to a friend.		
You have to be brave when you're scared.		

Post-Reading Activities

Culminating Activity: Stick Puppets and Reader's Theater

Directions: Reproduce the stick puppet patterns on pages 60–62 on tagboard or construction paper. Have students cut along the dashed lines. To complete the stick puppets, glue each pattern to a tongue depressor or craft stick.

Consider the following suggestions for using the stick puppets:

- Prepare the stick puppets to use with the reader's theater script on pages 63–64. Let small groups of students take turns reading the parts with the stick puppets.
- Let students experiment with the stick puppets by retelling the different Owl stories in their own words.
- Have students create new Owl adventures, using the stick puppets.
- If other characters are needed, have students make their own stick puppets.

Owl

Post-Reading Activities

Culminating Activity: Stick Puppets and Reader's Theater (cont.)

Mr. Turtle

Post-Reading Activities

Culminating Activity: Stick Puppets and Reader's Theater (cont.)

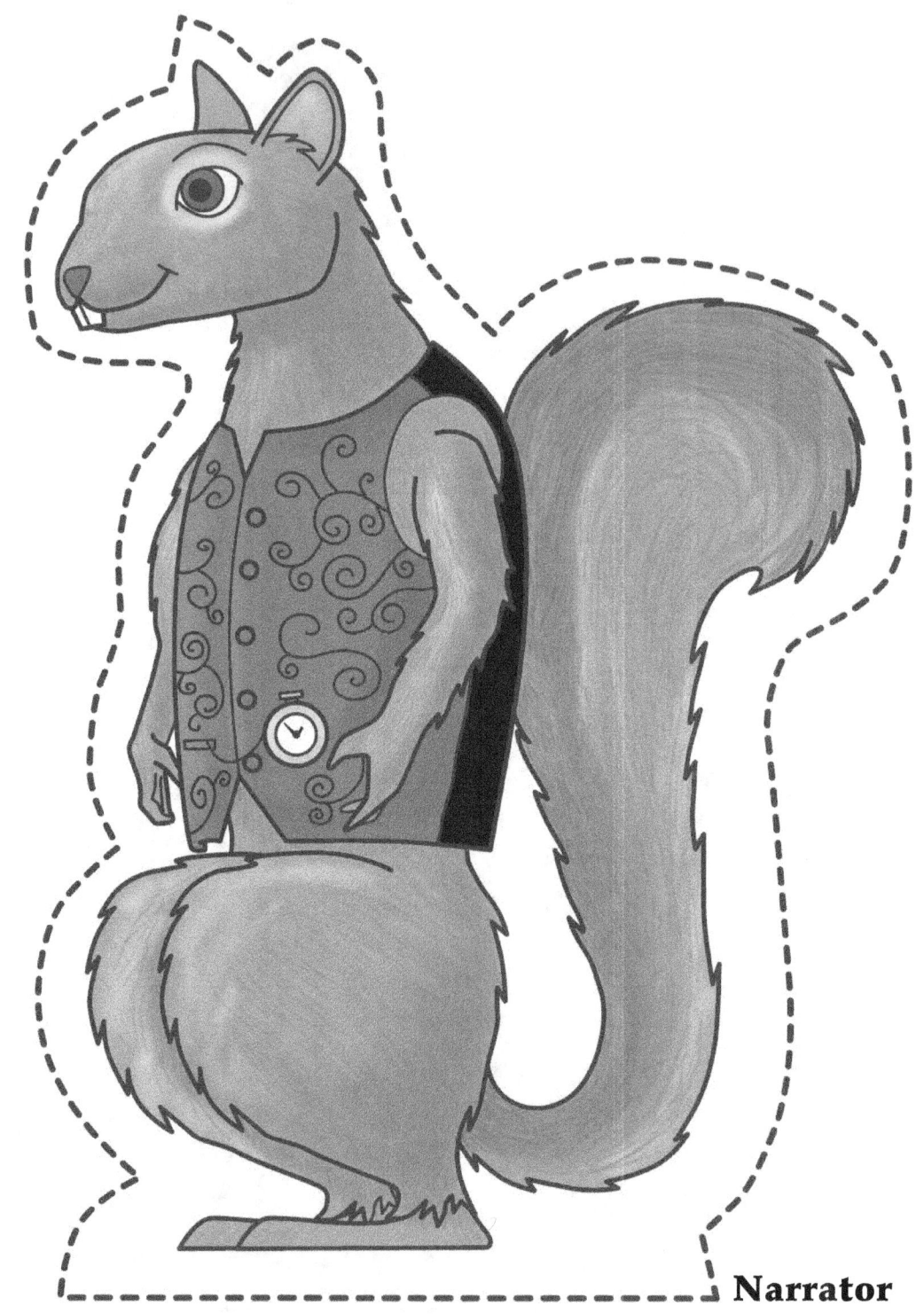

Narrator

Owl Meets a Friend

Characters

- Narrator
- Owl
- Mr. Turtle

Narrator: One bright spring day, Owl wakes up and has some breakfast.

Owl: It is such a nice day out! I think I will go for a walk.

Narrator: Owl grabs his coat and goes outside.

Owl: I wonder where I should walk today.

Narrator: Just then, Owl notices a turtle slowly walking by.

Owl: Hi, Mr. Turtle. How are you today?

Mr. Turtle: Very well, and yourself?

Owl: I was just going on a walk on this fine spring day.

Mr. Turtle: Oh, Owl, can I come with you?

Owl: Sure, I would be happy to have you join me.

Narrator: So, Owl and Mr. Turtle walk along the path by the river.

Owl: Let's have a race! Ready, set, go!

Post-Reading Activities

Owl Meets a Friend (cont.)

Narrator: Owl runs off, out of sight.

Mr. Turtle: I can't keep up!

Narrator: Turtle begins to cry. Owl hears crying from far away. Owl comes running back.

Owl: What is wrong, Mr. Turtle?

Mr. Turtle: You are too fast for me. I am just an old turtle.

Owl: I'm sorry, Mr. Turtle. I had no idea you couldn't keep up.

Mr. Turtle: It's okay, Owl. With all of these tears I am crying, I will make tear-water tea.

Narrator: Owl's face lit up.

Owl: Tear-water tea? That's my favorite. Let's go back to my home and make it together.

Mr. Turtle: That sounds wonderful, Owl.

Narrator: So, Owl and Mr. Turtle slowly walk to Owl's home to make tear-water tea.

Name _____

Post-Reading Activities

comprehension Assessment

Directions: Fill in the bubble for the best response to each question.

"The Guest"
1. Why does Owl tell Winter to go away and not come back?
   - (A) "It is so cold and snowy outside."
   - (B) "Owl was at home."
   - (C) "Soon everything was covered with snow."
   - (D) "Winter came into the house."

"Strange Bumps"
2. Why is Owl cold?
   - (A) The bump near his right foot moves up and down.
   - (B) Owl tries to go to sleep, but he cannot.
   - (C) Owl pulls the covers off his bed.
   - (D) Owl is in his bed.

"Tear-Water Tea"
3. Describe why Owl cries.

_____
_____
_____
_____

Post-Reading Activities

Comprehension Assessment (cont.)

"Upstairs and Downstairs"

4. What part tells us why Owl wants to be upstairs and downstairs at the same time?

   A) "Owl ran up the stairs."

   B) "I am always missing one place or the other."

   C) "Owl ran up and down the stairs faster and faster."

   D) "When I am down I am not up."

"Owl and the Moon"

5. Why does Owl think the moon is gone?

   A) The moon goes behind the clouds.

   B) His room is very dark.

   C) Owl does not feel sad anymore.

   D) He put his head on the pillow.

Name _____

Post-Reading Activities

Response to Literature: Lessons for Owl

Directions: Choose one of the Owl stories you've read. Think about which scene in the story is your very favorite. Draw a picture of that scene. Then, answer the questions on the next page about your scene. Make sure your picture is neat and is in color.

Post-Reading Activities

Name _____

Response to Literature: Lessons for Owl *(cont.)*

1. What is happening in the scene?
   _____
   _____
   _____
   _____

2. Why did you choose this scene?
   _____
   _____
   _____
   _____

3. What happens next in the story?
   _____
   _____
   _____
   _____

Name _____

Post-Reading Activities

Response to Literature Rubric

Directions: Use this rubric to evaluate student responses.

Great Job	Good Work	Keep Trying
☐ You answered all three questions completely. You included many details.	☐ You answered all three questions.	☐ You did not answer all three questions.
☐ Your handwriting is very neat. There are no spelling errors.	☐ Your handwriting can be neater. There are some spelling errors.	☐ Your handwriting is not very neat. There are many spelling errors.
☐ Your picture is neat and fully colored.	☐ Your picture is neat and some of it is colored.	☐ Your picture is not very neat and/or fully colored.
☐ Creativity is clear in both the picture and the writing.	☐ Creativity is clear in either the picture or the writing.	☐ There is not much creativity in either the picture or the writing.

Teacher Comments: _____

_____

_____

Writing Paper

Name _____

Answer Key

The responses provided here are just examples of what the students may answer. Many accurate responses are possible for the questions throughout this unit.

Vocabulary Activity—Section 1:
"The Guest" (page 15)
1. Winter is **banging** at Owl's door.

Guided Close Reading—Section 1:
"The Guest" (page 18)
1. "No one was there." and "Only the snow and the wind."
2. Some of the sensory words are banging, punching, knocking, and thumping.
3. Owl sits near the fire again.

Making Connections—Section 1:
"The Guest" (page 19)
The leaf, feather, and straw are items that will be blown by the wind (fan). The crayon may roll when the wind hits it.

Story Elements—Section 1:
"The Guest" (page 21)
The pictures and labels will vary but might include a cold wind pushing Owl against the wall; Winter running around the room; wind blowing out the fire in the fireplace; the snow whirling up the stairs; wind making the window shades flap and shiver; Winter turning the pea soup into hard, green ice; and everything covered with snow.

Vocabulary Activity—Section 2:
"Strange Bumps" (page 24)
- It is late, and Owl **yawns**.
- Owl blows out the **candle** to go to sleep.
- Owl sees two **strange** bumps at the bottom of his bed.
- The bumps **move** up and down.
- The bed falls down with a **crash** and a bang.
1. Owl decides to sleep in the chair where he feels **safe**.

Guided Close Reading—Section 2:
"Strange Bumps" (page 27)
1. Owl moves his right foot up and down and then moves his left foot up and down.
2. Owl pulls all the covers off of his bed.
3. Owl only sees his own two feet at the bottom of his bed.

Making Connections—Section 2:
"Strange Bumps" (page 28)
Questions will vary, but each should begin with *who*, *what*, *when*, or *where*.

Language Learning—Section 2:
"Strange Bumps" (page 29)
Sensory words will vary but might include: darkness, grows bigger, moving, crash, bang, and falling down.

Vocabulary Activity—Section 3:
"Tear-Water Tea" (page 33)
- "Owl took the **kettle** out of the **cupboard**."
- "He put the **kettle** on his **lap**."
- "'Chairs with **broken** legs,' said Owl."
- "Many large tears dropped into the **kettle**."
- "Soon the **kettle** was all **filled up** with tears."
- "He put the **kettle** on the stove to **boil** for tea."

Guided Close Reading—Section 3:
"Tear-Water Tea" (page 36)
1. Owl feels happy.
2. The tea tastes salty, but it is always good.
3. Owl stops crying because he is done thinking of sad things and it is time to boil the tea.

Making Connections—Section 3:
"Tear-Water Tea" (page 37)

Reuse	Recycle	Compost
empty egg carton, empty coffee can, water bottle	soda bottle, water bottle, empty egg carton	apple core, banana peel

Language Learning—Section 3:
"Tear-Water Tea" (page 38)
Things that make Owl sad will vary, but could include: chairs, songs, spoons, books, clocks, mornings, mashed potatoes, and pencils.

Answer Key

Vocabulary Activity—Section 4: "Upstairs and Downstairs" (page 42)
1. Sometimes Owl is **downstairs** in his living room.
2. Owl is always **missing** one place or another.
3. Owl runs upstairs and downstairs all **evening**.
4. Owl cannot be in both places **at once**.
5. Owl is **tired** because he keeps running up and down the stairs all evening.

Guided Close Reading—Section 4: "Upstairs and Downstairs" (page 45)
1. "There must be a way to be upstairs and downstairs at the same time."
2. Owl is always missing upstairs or downstairs.
3. Owl runs very fast to see if he can be in both places at once.

Making Connections—Section 4: "Upstairs and Downstairs" (page 46)
1. found
2. cold
3. short
4. right
5. under
6. off

Language Learning—Section 4: "Upstairs and Downstairs" (page 47)
- bedroom
- downstairs
- stairway
- upstairs

Story Elements—Section 4: "Upstairs and Downstairs" (page 49)
Drawings and predictions will vary, but they should show a clear prediction of what Owl would possibly do after resting on the middle of the stairs.

Vocabulary Activity—Section 5: "Owl and the Moon" (page 51)
1. Owl thinks the moon is following him because he is walking home and the moon is always there.

Guided Close Reading—Section 5: "Owl and the Moon" (page 54)
1. He doesn't think the moon hears him and he wants to say good-bye.
2. The moon disappears. The moon really just goes behind the clouds.
3. Owl is feeling "sad."

Making Connections—Section 5: "Owl and the Moon" (page 55)
Mooncake—There are three characters. Bear wants to take a bite of the moon. Bear tries to shoot a spoon at the moon. Bear makes a rocket ship to fly to the moon. Bear thinks he is on the moon. Bear thinks he is eating some of the moon, but it is really snow.

Similar—An animal is the main character. The main characters both sit down outside and look at the moon. The moon is a full moon.

"Owl and the Moon"—Owl and the moon are the only characters. Owl thinks the moon is his friend. Owl thinks the moon is following him.

Comprehension Assessment (pages 65–66)
1. C. "Soon everything was covered with snow."
2. C. Owl pulls the covers off his bed.
3. He thinks of many sad things. As he pictures each image in his head, he cries about it. The tears end up making him feel better.
4. B. "I am always missing one place or the other."
5. A. The moon goes behind the clouds.